WILDLIFE VIEWING AREAS

Oklahoma Ecoregions

- High Plains
- Southwestern Tablelands
- Central Great Plains
- Flint Hills
- Cross Timbers
- East Central Texas Plains
- South Central Plains
- Ouachita Mountains
- Arkansas Valley
- Boston Mountains
- Ozark Highlands
- Central Irregular Plains

1. Optima National Wildlife Refuge
2. Alabaster Caverns State Park
3. Salt Plains National Wildlife Refuge
4. Woolaroc Ranch, Museum & Wildlife Preserve
5. Oxley Nature Center
6. Bernice State Park
7. Greenleaf State Park
8. Deep Fork National Wildlife Refuge
9. Sam Noble Oklahoma Museum of Natural History
10. Sequoyah National Wildlife Refuge
11. Robbers Cave State Park
12. Robert S. Kerr Nature Center
13. Beavers Bend Nature Center
14. McGee Creek State Park
15. Boggy Depot State Park
16. Tishomingo National Wildlife Refuge
17. Lake Texoma State Park
18. Travertine Nature Center
19. Crow's Secret Nature Center
20. Martin Park Nature Center
21. Fort Cobb State Park
22. Hackberry Flat Wildlife Management Area
23. Quartz Mountain Nature Park
24. Washita National Wildlife Refuge

OKLAHOMA WILDLIFE
A Folding Pocket Guide to Familiar Animals

INVERTEBRATES

Honey Bee
Apis mellifera
To .75 in. (2 cm)
Slender bee has pollen baskets on its rear legs. Can only sting once. **Oklahoma's state insect.**

Paper Wasp
Polistes spp.
To 1 in. (3 cm)
Told by slender profile and dark, pale-banded abdomen. Builds papery hanging nests. Can sting repeatedly.

Bumble Bee
Bombus spp.
To 1 in. (3 cm)
Stout, furry bee is large and noisy. Can sting repeatedly.

Green Darner
Anax junius
To 3 in. (8 cm)
Has a bright green thorax and a blue body. Like most dragonflies, it rests with its wings open.

Ebony Jewelwing
Calopteryx maculata
To 1.75 in. (4.5 cm)
Like most damselflies, it rests with its wings held together over its back.

Ladybug Beetle
Family Coccinellidae
To .5 in. (1.3 cm)
Red wing covers are black-spotted.

Giant Stag Beetle
Lucanus elephus
To 2.5 in. (6 cm)

Whirligig Beetle
Gyrinus spp.
To .5 in. (1.3 cm)
Large swarms swirl around on the water's surface.

Water Strider
Gerris spp.
To .5 in. (1.3 cm)
Long-legged insect skates along the water's surface.

Cicada
Tibicen spp.
To 1.5 in. (4 cm)
Song is a sudden loud whine or buzz, maintained steadily before dying away.

Field Cricket
Gryllus pennsylvanicus
To 1 in. (3 cm)
Song is a series of 3 chirps.

Chigger (Velvet Mite)
Family Trombidiidae
To .12 in. (.3 cm)
Tiny, biting woodland insects leave red welts on human skin.

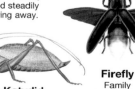

True Katydid
Pterophylla camellifolia
To 2 in. (5 cm)
Loud 2-part call – *katy-DID* – is heard on summer evenings.

Firefly
Family Lampyridae
To .6 in. (1.5 cm)

Fire Ant
Solenopsis geminata
To .25 in. (.6 cm)
Named for its painful, burning sting.

BUTTERFLIES

Black Swallowtail
Papilio polyxenes
To 3.5 in. (9 cm)
Oklahoma's state butterfly.

Cabbage White
Pieris rapae
To 2 in. (5 cm)
One of the most common butterflies.

Eastern Tiger Swallowtail
Papilio glaucus
To 6 in. (15 cm)

Eastern Tailed Blue
Everes comyntas
To 1 in. (3 cm)
Note orange spots above thread-like hindwing tails.

Mourning Cloak
Nymphalis antiopa
To 3.5 in. (9 cm)
Emerges during the first spring thaw.

Cloudless Sulphur
Phoebis sennae
To 3 in. (8 cm)
Common in open areas and fields.

Question Mark
Polygonia Interrogationis
To 2.5 in. (6 cm)
Note lilac margin on wings. Silvery mark on underwings resembles a question mark or semi-colon.

Buckeye
Junonia coenia
To 2.5 in. (6 cm)

Queen
Danaus gilippus
To 3.5 in. (9 cm)
Rich, brown-orange wings are finely spotted with white dots.

Red Admiral
Vanessa atalanta
To 2.5 in. (6 cm)

Pearly Crescentspot
Phyciodes tharos
To 1.5 in. (4 cm)
Hindwing is marked with dark crescent-shaped spots.

Zebra Longwing
Heliconius charithonia
To 3.5 in. (9 cm)

Common Checkered Skipper
Pyrgus communis
To 1.25 in. (3.2 cm)

Monarch
Danaus plexippus
To 4 in. (10 cm)

Viceroy
Limenitis archippus
To 3 in. (8 cm)
Told from similar monarch by its smaller size and the thin, black band on its hindwings.

FISHES

Rainbow Trout
Oncorhynchus mykiss To 44 in. (1.1 m)
Note reddish side stripe.

Brown Trout
Salmo trutta To 40 in. (1 m)
Has red and black spots on its body.

Crappie
Pomoxis spp. To 20 in. (50 cm)

Channel Catfish
Ictalurus punctatus To 4 ft. (1.2 m)
Note prominent "whiskers."

Redear Sunfish
Lepomis microlophus To 14 in. (35 cm)

Flathead Catfish
Pylodictis olivaris To 5 ft. (1.5 m)
Head is long and flat.

Bluegill
Lepomis macrochirus To 16 in. (40 cm)

Largemouth Bass
Micropterus salmoides To 40 in. (1 m)
Note prominent side spots. Jaw joint extends past eye.

White Bass
Morone chrysops To 18 in. (45 cm)
Silvery fish has 4-7 dark side stripes. **Oklahoma's state fish.**

Smallmouth Bass
Micropterus dolomieu To 27 in. (68 cm)
Jaw joint is beneath the eye.

Hybrid Bass
Morone hybrid To 20 in. (50 cm)
Note broken side stripes. Striped and white bass hybrid is an aggressive sport fish.

Striped Bass
Morone saxatilis To 6 ft. (1.8 m)
Has 6-9 dark side stripes.

Walleye
Sander vitreus To 40 in. (1 m)
Note white spot on lower lobe of tail.

Longnose Gar
Lepisosteus osseus
To 6 ft. (1.8 m)

REPTILES & AMPHIBIANS

    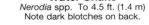   

Bullfrog
Lithobates catesbeianus
To 8 in. (20 cm)
Call is a deep-pitched – *jurrrooom*
Oklahoma's state amphibian.

Chorus Frog
Pseudacris triseriata
To 1.5 in. (4 cm)
Note dark stripes on back. Call sounds like running a thumbnail over the teeth of a comb.

Gray Treefrog
Hyla versicolor
To 2.5 in. (6 cm)
Call is a short, resonating trill.

Red-eared Slider
Trachemys scripta elegans
To 11 in. (28 cm)

Snapping Turtle
Chelydra serpentina To 18 in. (45 cm)
Note knobby shell and long tail.

Prairie Lizard
Sceloporus undulatus consobrinus
To 8 in. (20 cm)
Note light side stripes.

Box Turtle
Terrapene spp.
To 9 in. (23 cm)
Note high-domed shell.

Collared Lizard
Crotaphytus collaris To 14 in. (35 cm)
Note 2 dark collar markings.
Oklahoma's state reptile.

Texas Horned Lizard
Phrynosoma cornutum
To 7 in. (18 cm)

Corn Snake
Pantherophis guttatus To 6 ft. (1.8 m)
Told by black-bordered, red blotches.

Water Snake
Nerodia spp. To 4.5 ft. (1.4 m)
Note dark blotches on back.

Common Garter Snake
Thamnophis sirtalis sirtalis
To 4 ft. (1.2 m)
Has yellowish back and side stripes. Color and pattern are variable.

Timber Rattlesnake
Crotalus horridus To 6 ft. (1.8 m)
Note black tail. Venomous.

Copperhead
Agkistrodon contortrix To 52 in. (1.3 m)
Venomous snake has hourglass-shaped bands down its back.

BIRDS

Canada Goose
Branta canadensis
To 45 in. (1.14 m)

Mallard
Anas platyrhynchos To 28 in. (70 cm)

Killdeer
Charadrius vociferus
To 12 in. (30 cm)

Wood Duck
Aix sponsa To 20 in. (50 cm)

Great Egret
Ardea alba
To 38 in. (95 cm)
Note yellow bill
and black feet.

Cattle Egret
Bubulcus ibis
To 20 in.
(50 cm)

Snowy Egret
Egretta thula
To 26 in. (65 cm)
Note black bill
and yellow feet.

Double-crested Cormorant
Phalacrocorax auritus
To 3 ft. (90 cm)

American White Pelican
Pelecanus erythrorhynchos
To 5 ft. (1.5 m)

Ring-billed Gull
Larus delawarensis
To 20 in. (50 cm)
Bill has dark ring.

Sandhill Crane
Antigone canadensis
To 4 ft. (1.2 m)

Turkey Vulture
Cathartes aura
To 32 in. (80 cm)
Note red head and
two-toned underwings.

Red-tailed Hawk
Buteo jamaicensis
To 25 in. (63 cm)

Bald Eagle
Haliaeetus leucocephalus
To 40 in. (1 m)

BIRDS

American Kestrel
Falco sparverius
To 12 in. (30 cm)

Barred Owl
Strix varia
Call is a loud –
who-cooks-for-you?
who-cooks-for-you-all?
To 2 ft. (60 cm)

Great Horned Owl
Bubo virginianus
To 25 in. (63 cm)
Call is a resonant –
hoo-HOO-hoooo.

Mourning Dove
Zenaida macroura
To 13 in. (33 cm)
Call is a mournful –
ooah-woo-woo-woo.

Ruby-throated Hummingbird
Archilochus colubris
To 3.5 in. (9 cm)

Wild Turkey
Meleagris gallopavo
To 4 ft. (1.2 m)
Oklahoma's state
game bird.

Rock Pigeon
Columba livia
To 13 in. (33 cm)

Yellow-billed Cuckoo
Coccyzus americanus
To 14 in. (35 cm)

Ring-necked Pheasant
Phasianus colchicus
To 3 ft. (90 cm)

Northern Bobwhite
Colinus virginianus
To 12 in. (30 cm)

Greater Roadrunner
Geococcyx californianus
To 2 ft. (60 cm)

Tufted Titmouse
Baeolophus bicolor
To 6 in. (15 cm)

Carolina Wren
Thryothorus ludovicianus
To 6 in. (15 cm)

Belted Kingfisher
Megaceryle alcyon
To 14 in. (35 cm)

BIRDS

Northern Flicker
Colaptes auratus
To 13 in. (33 cm)
Wing and tail
linings are yellow.

Pileated Woodpecker
Dryocopus pileatus
To 17 in. (43 cm)
Note large size.

Hairy Woodpecker
Dryobates villosus
To 10 in. (25 cm)

Scissor-tailed Flycatcher
Tyrannus forficatus
To 14 in. (35 cm)
Oklahoma's
state bird.

Purple Martin
Progne subis
To 8 in. (20 cm)

Barn Swallow
Hirundo rustica
To 8 in. (20 cm)
Note deeply forked tail.

Carolina Chickadee
Poecile carolinensis
To 4.5 in. (11 cm)
Song is a whistled
– fee-bee fee-bay.

American Robin
Turdus migratorius
To 11 in. (28 cm)

Blue Jay
Cyanocitta cristata
To 14 in. (35 cm)

White-breasted Nuthatch
Sitta carolinensis
To 6 in. (15 cm)

Baltimore Oriole
Icterus galbula
To 8 in. (20 cm)

Indigo Bunting
Passerina cyanea
To 6 in. (15 cm)

Western Meadowlark
Sturnella neglecta
To 9 in. (23 cm)

Eastern Bluebird
Sialia sialis
To 7 in. (18 cm)

Cedar Waxwing
Bombycilla cedrorum
To 7 in. (18 cm)

Evening Grosbeak
Coccothraustes vespertinus
To 8 in. (20 cm)

BIRDS

Red-winged Blackbird
Agelaius phoeniceus
To 9 in. (23 cm)

American Crow
Corvus brachyrhynchos
To 22 in. (55 cm)

Common Grackle
Quiscalus quiscula
To 14 in. (35 cm)

Northern Mockingbird
Mimus polyglottos
To 11 in. (28 cm)

Brown-headed Cowbird
Molothrus ater
To 7 in. (18 cm)

European Starling
Sturnus vulgaris
To 8 in. (20 cm)

House Sparrow
Passer domesticus
To 6 in. (15 cm)

American Goldfinch
Spinus tristis
To 5 in. (13 cm)

Dark-eyed Junco
Junco hyemalis
To 7 in. (18 cm)

Eastern Towhee
Pipilo erythrophthalmus
To 9 in. (23 cm)

Common Yellowthroat
Geothlypis trichas
To 5 in. (13 cm)

Northern Cardinal
Cardinalis cardinalis
To 9 in. (23 cm)

MAMMALS

Mexican Free-tailed Bat
Tadarida brasiliensis
To 5 in. (13 cm)
Oklahoma's state
flying mammal.

Virginia Opossum
Didelphis virginiana
To 40 in. (1 m)

Eastern Cottontail
Sylvilagus floridanus
To 18 in. (45 cm)

MAMMALS

Black-tailed Jackrabbit
Lepus californicus
To 25 in. (63 cm)
Tail and ears are
black-tipped.

Fox Squirrel
Sciurus niger
To 28 in. (70 cm)
Note large size.

Swamp Rabbit
Sylvilagus aquaticus
To 22 in. (55 cm)

Deer Mouse
Peromyscus maniculatus
To 8 in. (20 cm)
Has white undersides
and hairy tail.

Thirteen-lined Ground Squirrel
Spermophilus tridecemlineatus
To 12 in. (30 cm)

Eastern Gray Squirrel
Sciurus carolinensis
To 20 in. (50 cm)

Woodchuck
Marmota monax
To 32 in. (80 cm)

American Badger
Taxidea taxus
To 35 in. (88 cm)

Black-tailed Prairie Dog
Cynomys ludovicianus
To 16 in. (40 cm)
Tail is black-tipped.

Norway Rat
Rattus norvegicus
To 18 in. (45 cm)

Nine-banded Armadillo
Dasypus novemcinctus
To 32 in. (80 cm)

Ringtail
Bassariscus astutus
To 30 in. (75 cm)

American Beaver
Castor canadensis
To 4 ft. (1.2 m)

Common Muskrat
Ondatra zibethicus
To 2 ft. (60 cm)

MAMMALS

Common Raccoon
Procyon lotor
To 28 in. (70 cm)
Oklahoma's state
furbearer animal.

Long-tailed Weasel
Mustela frenata
To 21 in. (53 cm)

Striped Skunk
Mephitis mephitis
To 32 in. (80 cm)

Bobcat
Lynx rufus
To 4 ft. (1.2 m)

Common Gray Fox
Urocyon cinereoargenteus
To 3.5 ft. (1.1 m)

Red Fox
Vulpes vulpes
To 40 in. (1 m)

Coyote
Canis latrans To 52 in. (1.3 m)

Pronghorn
Antilocapra americana
To 5 ft. (1.5 m)
Note "pronged" horns.

Wild Hog
Sus scrofa To 6 ft. (1.8 m)

American Bison
Bos bison To 12 ft. (3.6 m)
Oklahoma's state mammal.

White-tailed Deer
Odocoileus virginianus
To 7 ft. (2.1 m)
Oklahoma's state
game animal.